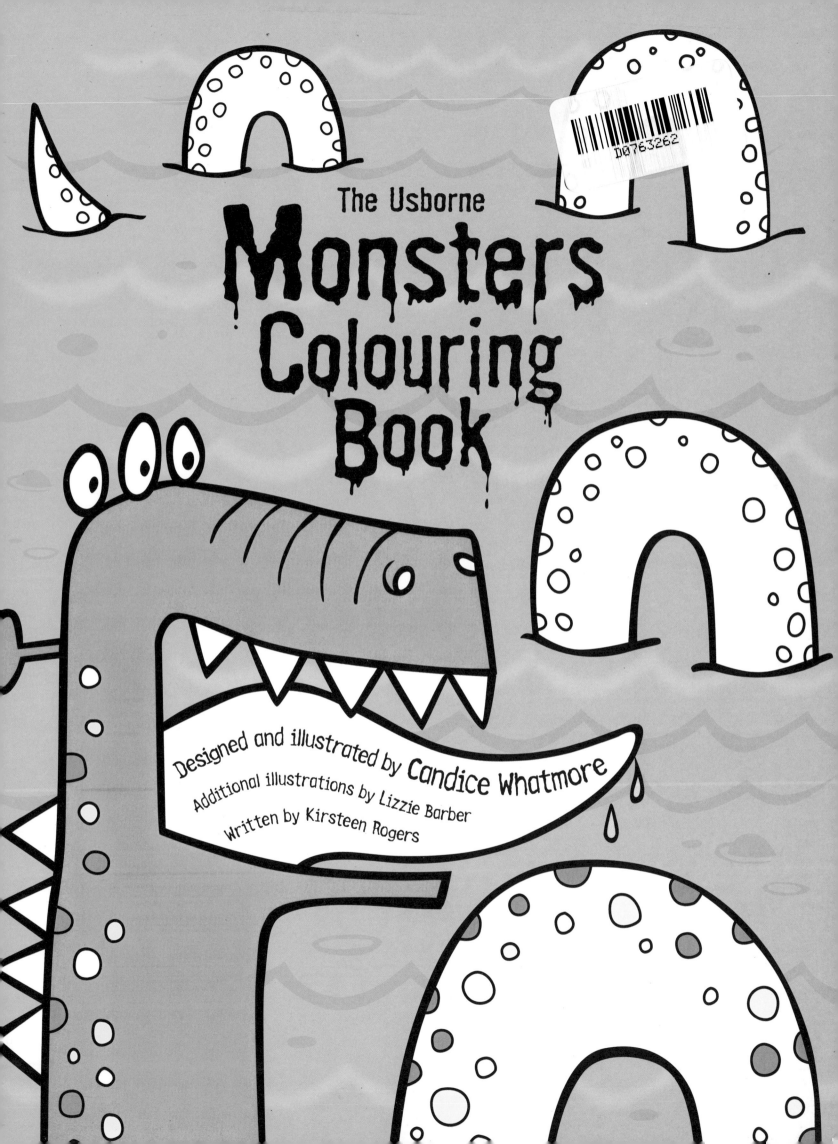

The Usborne Monsters Colouring Book

Designed and illustrated by **Candice Whatmore**

Additional illustrations by Lizzie Barber

Written by Kirsteen Rogers

Howling werewolves

As a bright, full moon rises over Creepy Canyon, the eerie yowling of a lone werewolf echoes across the emptiness. Suddenly another chilling howl answers the call, followed by another... and then another...

Here's a space for you to add a fourth fearsome werewolf to the pack – half man and half wolf, armed with razor-sharp claws.

How to draw a werewolf

Use a pencil to draw a large square

Draw a triangle

Add a semi-circle, then another smaller one inside

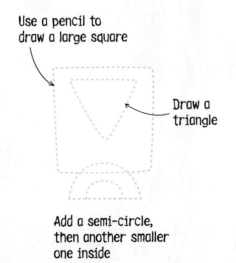

Draw two ears

Add two arms

Draw two feet

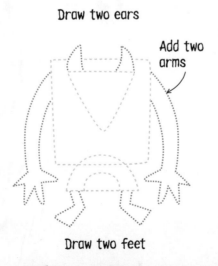

Use a pen to draw around the outline

Draw eyes, nose and mouth

Add claws to the hands and feet

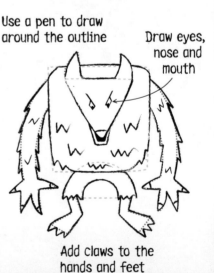

Monster in the city

Run for your life! An angry monster is rampaging through the city, bulldozing buildings, tearing up trees and crushing cars. Finish the cityscape below, adding sleek skyscrapers, and a few toppling towers. You could draw some cars, buses or trains too if you like.

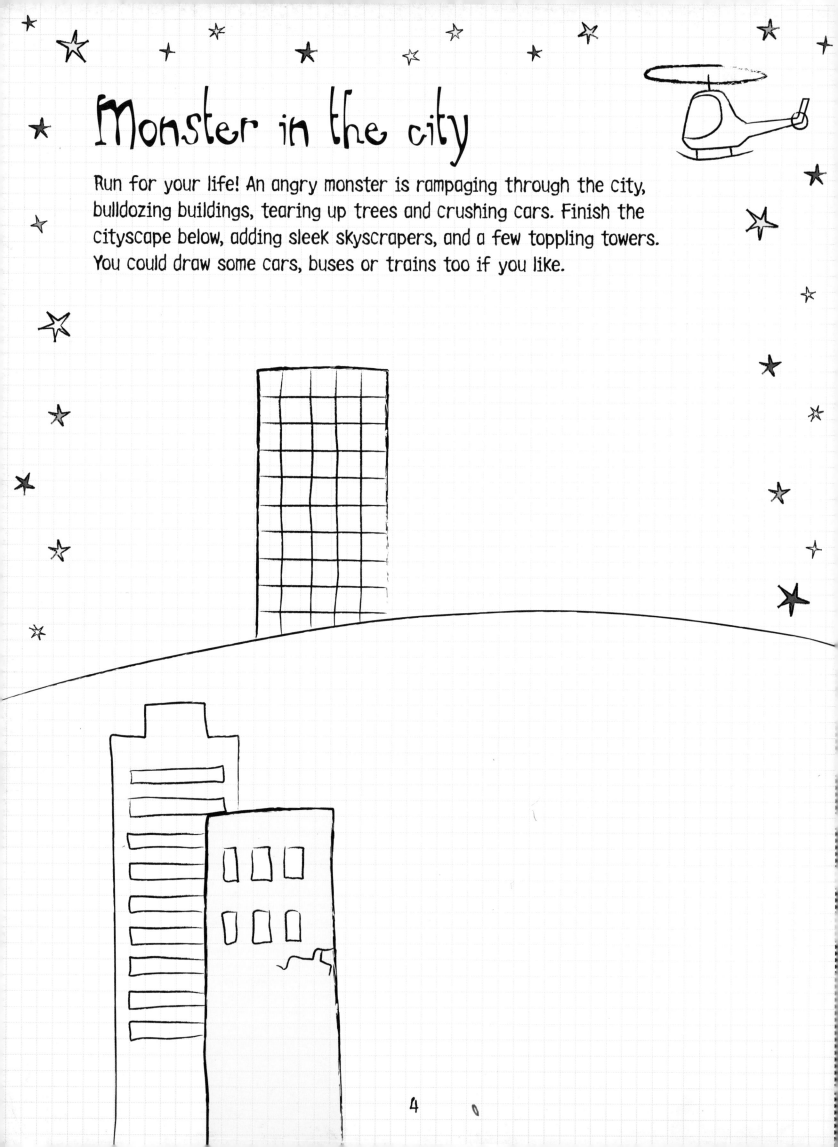

Swamp monster

In the great, green, greasy marshes lurks a hideous beast.
Covered in sludge and slime, the swamp monster lies in wait
for anyone who stumbles into its boggy den. Give this monster
eyes and a mouth, then draw some drips and other dribbly details.

Loch Ness Monster

Many look for it, a few claim to have seen it, but does it really exist? Is there an ancient McMonster living in the deep, dark waters of this Scottish Loch, or is it just a floating log, mistaken in the mists?

Draw your own "Nessie" in the space below.

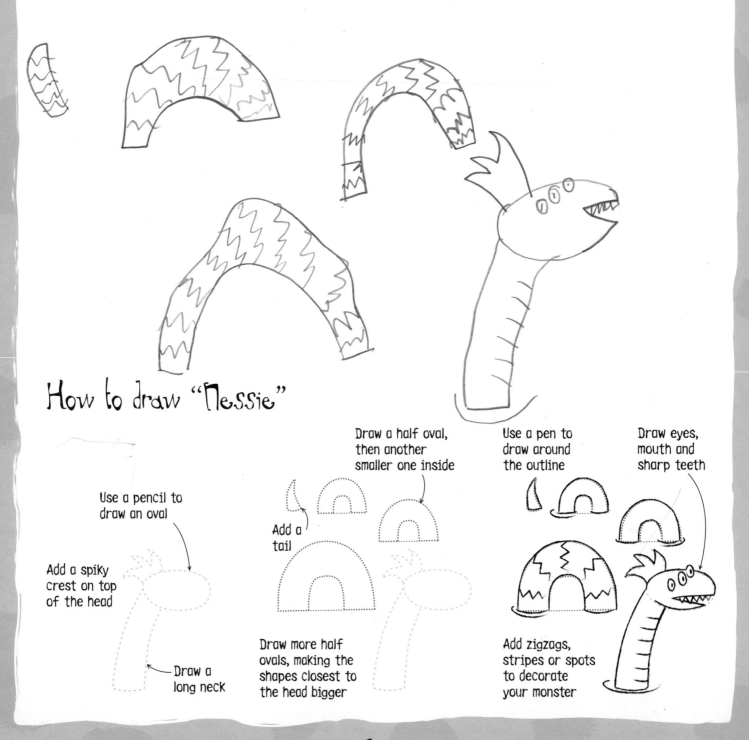

How to draw "Nessie"

Use a pencil to draw an oval

Add a spiky crest on top of the head

Draw a long neck

Add a tail

Draw more half ovals, making the shapes closest to the head bigger

Draw a half oval, then another smaller one inside

Use a pen to draw around the outline

Add zigzags, stripes or spots to decorate your monster

Draw eyes, mouth and sharp teeth

Hungry monster

RRRaaaarrrr! What deafening rumbles are thundering from this monster's tummy!
It is raiding the larder and will eat everything it sees to satisfy its hunger.
Write a menu for a mighty meal that a ravenous monster might like to munch.

Monster menu

Starters _____

_____

_____

_____

Main
courses _____

_____

_____

_____

Desserts _____

_____

_____

_____

Mini-monsters

Not all monsters are big, bold and brash – some are nasty little critters, so small that you might easily miss them. Create your own monster mini-beast garden by adding eyes, bodies and nippy gnashers to the shapes below.

Monster mug shots

This motley collection of criminals is wanted by the Ministry of Monsters for all sorts of mischief. Have you seen them? Read their Grime Squad files, then finish the identity cards below, based on the descriptions and pictures.

MINISTRY OF MONSTERS

MINISTRY OF MONSTERS
SPOTTY McDOTTY
USING SOAP

MINISTRY OF MONSTERS
SOCK MONSTER
REUNITING ODD SOCKS
IN THE LAUNDRY

MINISTRY OF MONSTERS

MINISTRY OF MONSTERS
TARANTULA GARGANTULA
RUNNING FROM A SCREAMING CHILD

MINISTRY OF MONSTERS
EVIL EYEBALL
BLINKING UNDER PRESSURE

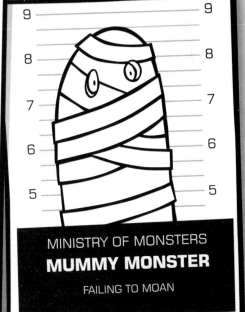

MINISTRY OF MONSTERS
MUMMY MONSTER
FAILING TO MOAN

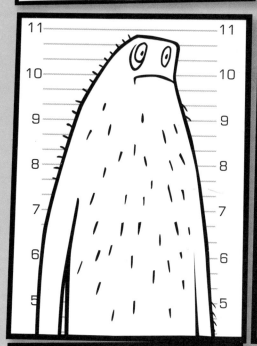

MINISTRY OF MONSTERS
DOPPLE CLANGER
RANDOM ACTS OF KINDNESS

MINISTRY OF MONSTERS
BEASTIE BLUBBER BLOB
ALLOWING HIMSELF
TO BE FLUSHED AWAY

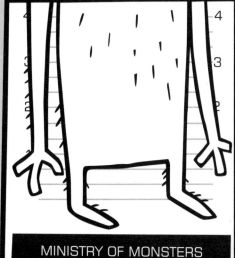

MINISTRY OF MONSTERS
TICKLE MONSTER
WARMING HANDS BEFORE DUTY

MINISTRY OF MONSTERS
MUNCHER CRUNCHER
GOING ON A DIET

MINISTRY OF MONSTERS
BRIAN
USING AN
UN-MONSTERLY NAME

Terrible troll

Some fairytales and legends tell of ugly monsters called trolls that live in dark, damp places – under dank bridges or in deep mountain caves. Some stories say that even a ray of sunlight turns them to stone. Trolls are incredibly strong, but rather smelly, slow and not very bright.

Draw some gruesome ingredients in the troll stew below.
The stinkier and more revolting they look, the better.

Monsters under the bed

Tired out by a day of naughtiness, sneaky Spike falls asleep. Almost at once, there's a rustle, then a groan, and one by one all kinds of monsters creep out from under his bed. There's Boggle-eyes the bookworm, and Snatch the thief, Moping Murgatroyd, and the tiresome Two-headed Tweak...

You could use this space to write
a story about what they did.

"Hey!" said Boggle-eyes, "Give that book back!"
"Shan't!" said Snatch, his . . . .
eyes glinting. "I want to look at the . . . .

. . . .

. . . .

. . . .

. . . .

. . . .

. . . .

The end

Alien monsters

Far out in space there may be all kinds of creatures, far stranger than anyone can imagine. Draw your own aliens in the spaceships below. There is space for you to design a spacecraft too.

Monsters in the attic

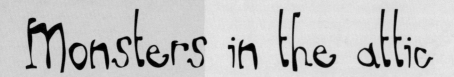

The attic is alive with mischievous monsters – muddle monsters who move things and brittle monsters who break things. Continue filling this attic room with junk. Then, add your own meddlesome monsters hiding amidst the mess.

Frankenstein's monster

Victor Frankenstein was a character in a storybook. He was an inventor who longed to find the secret of life. After years of experiments he built a creature out of spare parts and jolted it into life with a lightning flash. But his lumbering creation was so ugly that everyone feared it, and the lonely monster lived an empty life of bitter revenge.

How to draw Frankenstein's monster

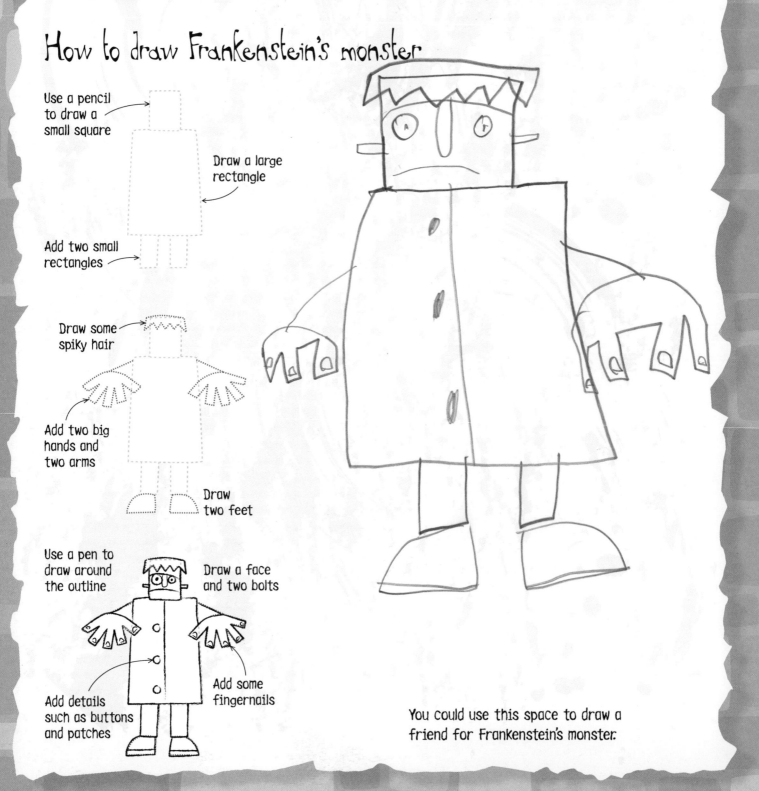

Use a pencil to draw a small square

Draw a large rectangle

Add two small rectangles

Draw some spiky hair

Add two big hands and two arms

Draw two feet

Use a pen to draw around the outline

Draw a face and two bolts

Add some fingernails

Add details such as buttons and patches

You could use this space to draw a friend for Frankenstein's monster.

Monster gallery

You don't have to go far to find a story with a monster in it. On the page opposite you can read about some famous monsters in myths and legends.

You could draw your own monster in the frame below. If you like, you could write about it too, for example, what is it called, what does it guard, and how can it be defeated?

HYDRA

In Greek myths, the Hydra was a terrible monster that lived in a dreary swamp. The creature had nine serpent-like heads which belched out billowing clouds of poison. A hero named Hercules was tasked to tackle the terror, but each time he swiped one of its heads with his club, two new heads grew in its place. His nephew used burning branches to set fire to its necks, and as the last head tumbled to the ground, so the Hydra was slain.

Dracula

Count Dracula is a vampire character in a book by Bram Stoker. Vampires are legendary monsters that steal life by drinking their victims' blood. They can be held at bay by garlic, holy water and the sign of the cross, which they cannot bear. But the only way to destroy a vampire is to drive a sharp wooden stake through its heart.

MANTICORE

This mythical monster from ancient Persia had the body of a lion, the head of a human, and three rows of savage teeth. It devoured its prey whole.

THE GOLEM

Golems are hulking creatures from Jewish legend, shaped from clay and brought to life by magic. The most famous one was the Golem of Prague.

Medusa

In Greek myths, Medusa was a hideous monster with seething snakes for hair. Anyone who looked at her turned to stone. A hero named Perseus sought her out and, by watching her reflection in his shiny shield, cut off her head.

Kraken

Kraken are legendary sea monsters that were once said to lurk in the chilly waters near Norway. Early accounts tell how these ocean giants reared up out of the waves, their thick tentacles thrashing, before sinking into the deep, leaving a whirl of rushing waters that sucked helpless ships down to their doom.

Add more long, lashing legs to this Kraken, then doodle some whirling waves around it.

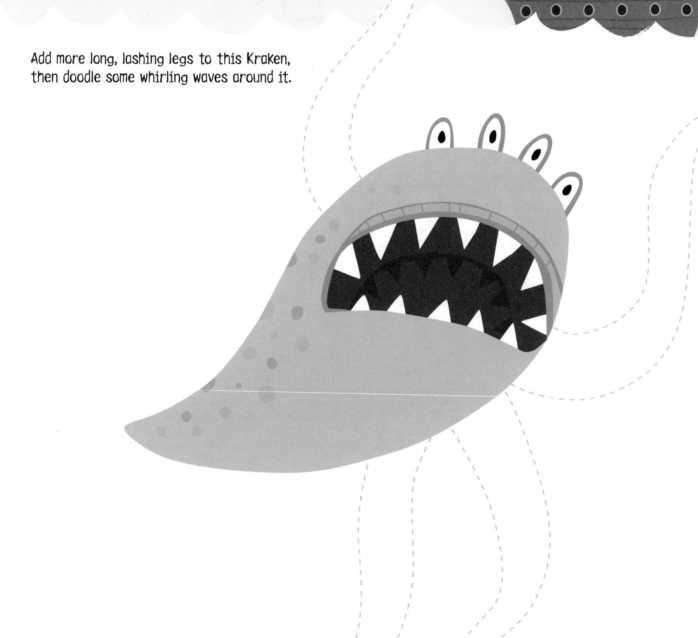

The Minotaur

The Minotaur was a terrible monster in Ancient Greek myths. Half bull and half man, it lurked at the heart of a labyrinth (a huge maze), devouring anyone who entered its lair. Eventually, a brave hero named Theseus destroyed the Minotaur, then escaped from the labyrinth by following a trail of enchanted twine.

Use your pencil to help Theseus find his way out of the labyrinth.

Colouring hints and tips

Use felt-tip pens or coloured pencils to colour in the pictures. Felt-tip pens will give you strong colours, while pencils will have a softer effect.

You can draw patterns within some of the shapes. For example, this scene is decorated with...

...zigzags and stripes...

If you want to cut out your picture, you'll find a dotted line on each page to cut along.

...waves and wiggles...

You could finish this picture to practise colouring.

...spots and dots.

It's a good idea to lay your book on a flat surface while you are colouring, or slip a piece of cardboard under the page you are filling in, to make a firm surface.

Fill in larger areas such as this table with lots of lines going in the same direction.

First published in 2011 by Usborne Publishing Ltd. 83–85 Saffron Hill, London EC1N 8RT, England. Copyright ©2011 Usborne Publishing Ltd. The name Usborne and the devices ♀ 🜨 are Trade Marks of Usborne Publishing Ltd. All rights reserved. No part of this publication may be reproduced, stored in a retrieval system, or transmitted in any form or by any means, electronic, mechanical, photocopying, recording or otherwise, without the prior permission of the publisher. Printed in Dongguan, Guangdong, China.